ON THE EDGE OF A MIRROR

LEE GOLDSTEIN

Volume 1 (3rd edition)

Chapbook Press

Schuler Books
2660 28th Street SE
Grand Rapids, MI 49512
(616) 942-7330
www.schulerbooks.com

On the Edge of a Mirror – Volume 1

3rd edition

ISBN 13: 9781948237901

Library of Congress Control Number: 2021919141

Printed in the United States by Chapbook Press.

Dedication

The manuscript of this book was composed
amid the horns
of a dilemma
and as a circumstance of alienation
for the author.

To those people, who most helped him
see this work through to completion
and to legitimize his work,
the book is dedicated.

To Evelyn Goldstein, Dolores Granger, Curtis Brooks, Jay Dillon,
Roger and Ellen Jones, Carole Bryan—and Evie Green and the
Topeka Write Stuff authors group—and to the wise editorship of
Kristen Robbs and Ann Brooks.

In acknowledgment to journals I have been published in:

The Deronda Review

Transcendent Visions

The American Dissident

Exquisite Corpse

Humanistic Mathematics Network Journal

Mathematical Intelligencer

Reflect

Foreword

It has been said that the true artist lives in the metaphysical. It has
also been said that the mathematician has a reality that transcends
the human mind. Mr. Goldstein, being both poet and
mathematician, has produced a work that clearly embodies these
two concepts.

With amusement, he sometimes refers to it as a nonorthology of
blemishes. But those who understand it will approach knowing
what he knows and perhaps arrive a little closer to the unknown
places that exist within us.

Dolores Granger, Poet, Musician

Table of Contents

Elopement of the Words

I listened, intent,
to the words of his speech.
These words were like slinks
that languish
in a mock of the place
of their detention,
punishing speakers,
who use such words
for their own obscurity.

Mind

Cavitation

A descent into the cave
of the poem,
when it has been written at a place
with momentary slippage--
a place associated with the sense
of a person beside himself,
or of people aside themselves
to one availing of only half his own diction
and the other half after the fact.

Reality

Is reality restricted
to behaviors in time
and is this, in fact,
living in actuality?
You do not believe
in behaviors *out of time,*
but neither do you live
in actuality,
even if you don't admit it.

Foghorn

One becomes conditioned
in an argument to talk,
even now, on a roll
without sufficient restraint
until he becomes blue in the face,
like a foghorn
on the expanse of the oceans,
and he,
like the signal, in toto.

Carpe Diem

In your solicitous intent
to improve my day,
I'd rather just say,
"Aid me to get through the day.
Otherwise, don't help me at all."
For at present I haven't a *carte blanche* interest
in so grand a conversion by you
or anyone else's particular
point of view.

Stylus

My confession:
That, sometimes, I feel like a stylus,
a sponge,
or a needle, astringed
to the here and now,
intensely, either duplicating such quoins of reality,
or neutral,
contributing to the world
after almost blanching in it.

The Fifth Dimension

I cannot see
what is so anti-pole unequal
with what is at hand
in the focus of my mind
or as not immediate
of the regressive contingency,
that I may compromise myself or my thoughts,
but for the veridical explorer
of the potential of the mind.

Discrepant

These are times
that may foster
a breaking up
of one's psychic outlay:
That a wanton world may allure us
and reify our human susceptibilities,
to picture, to fable,
or spell us,
and to leave us halfway in emptiness.

Chat Room

It's the devil
who could give
modern man
his rubric
in these critical times,
with a person's
ethical issues
like a chat room
in a fill of these devils.

Negative Introspection

The devil says,
"You are a self-invalidation,
and if you have any
existential qualities at all,
then you are for me."
Or like the devil's other minions,
those precipitated in this way:
They have sold-out, having patently
compromised in their own hubris.

Ben's Element

Ben speaks the language of the Oorts,
people, who live on ice balls
in the Oort cloud,
billions of miles from the sun.
Or many of the
earth people of late
should leave Ben to his element,
or left behind,
to boot.

Confixations

It is through
a focus in healing;
the confixations--
Or the others' dialogue
to contend with others' genetic ignorance,
I can resume
with a trust and the understanding
by which I could obtain
to be quite so much the better.

Incapability

We may tend to support
people incapacitated
before we support
people of incapability.
For the latter suggests itself as hindering
the next person,
while the former
might lend itself
more to the state of your sympathies.

Impredicable

The illness,
coruscant of my brain,
but leaves my mind unshackled:
And my mind
can know the illness absolutely,
but every explanation
I could give of it
can come out sounding
like a subjectivity.

Wizards

Most people don't believe
in living in actuality.
Some are the nominalists,
accused by the realists.
Some people do live
in actuality,
or only be disregarded
by the nominalists
for being wizards.

Dis-privatied

It can be said of one's "star chamber",
perdures between times.

Troubled by the others' surveillance,
little privacy
remains a circumstance,
is one banned
from furthering
the practice
of the left hand
not knowing
what the right hand is doing.

Depression

In this contingency,
few remain interested in his personal reflections
of the world, to the decline of his appeal
or in the neglect of himself
like the bite of a snake,
which instead of those moments' fruitfulness,
or his soul
be turned into stone.

There are the occasions of
what can be the regress
from a quasi-consciousness,
or of an altered and a belittled experience,
a primitivity of depressiveness,
or that could be like entities
living in a strangeness
of the so-called states of depression.

The Noise

The depressive person,
or in his compensations,
might be like
a subliminal striping,
or heard in the darkness,
too unsubtle
for a conventional hearing,
even of his own regress.

Forest for the Trees

A more level-minded person
could discern a threshold
of sometimes the portion
and sometimes the whole,
a balance between the trees
and the forest,
alternately one or the other
select or sighted,
even in the wisdom of the choice.

Aloneness

To practice one's time
being alone,
even for the sake of one's art,
or a wanton aloneness
and a risk
of the metaphysical seams
in the weaving
of the thread of loneness
and what is not compromised by another.

The Sticking Place

Life's a game
of outliers,
ever there be inliers
sticking to outliers
and the passion
to become a pulsion
in whose parts
of these times,
forever the challenge.

Shadower

It is in the best interest
not to remain indifferent
to the cultural shadowing
of spirited people
and the shadows
on the wall
of Plato's cave
could be a projection or shades
in Hades.

Conciliation

I have honored you
in a drifting
of the cooperation,
at least, of being
the pretty leaves that fall at random,
or some blown into my backyard,
every now and then,
and in whatever currency of the airing
ought to admit.

He

Like a thief
in the night,
he composes his poems,
as though
they were
a metaphysical relation
of himself
to the egotistical world.

Shakespeare

'Negative capability':
Keats's term
could ascribe the aesthetic
in Shakespeare,
as over Iago in the play, *Othello,*
that prefers to transcend
a 'negative order of evaluation'
in a grace
above the latter.

Nonselection

Nothing's special
about my coming into your life
to help you out
when you were younger
in Boulder
in the 1990's.
If not me,
someone else could have come
in my stead.

A Subject

A toxic noise from the wasteland
comes suctioning
from the honeycombed slack of the vast,
minus an object of certainty--
A plumbed form, no more than this,
escaping the depression
of an emptiness
in one niche or another,
unless if caught by a Windigo.

Nightmare

Language's use in life
is like a kangaroo court:
Hapless in 'contempt of court',
a breach,
and in a legitimate court
is an irrelative intention,
or a cut-short attention
to the proceedings of the court
in my bad dreams.

Insomnia

Of a groping discomfort at night,
in not falling asleep--
And, ultimately, to carry
some worries,
while in the preference
to be asleep--
Or make a vigil, instead of sleep--
Even to be like
ever as not to fall asleep.

Elusion

The refusal to be eluded
in the face of the truth
of life interests,
the person isn't there,
less a contrast
of my going out
on a limb for Him,
or the truth is, again,
He isn't there!

Synthetic Joy

Coca Cola, Pepsi Cola, et al.,
as complementary, or compensative
an exuberance
in one's humor,
or the occasion
of those drinks
for nausea,
or a cure
for a modest dyspepsia.

Pornography, et al.

To alter
from the refinement
of a tried convention of culture,
a mannered behavior
for many people:
And his conduct having gone lax, too,
or notwithstanding,
a shrinkage
of the brain.

Envy

Whose dissatisfaction's case scenario:
One personally
is ill-at-ease
in what he does not possess,
or an urgent anticipation,
and another not having offered,
or his chagrin in not having received
of another
unto himself.

Pliancy

You could see me
on an ocean-going vessel,
shifting winds, as they are,
and I, a refuse to the vast,
as incompliant
of being an aid to the want in me
and in turn when you may not have a designation--
Or in your own time,
to relate to me.

Pathos

As unceasing a pathos,
a response,
or like an illusion
without the material world,
and this
could be hoaxed,
or unscientific,
being before
the "last wave".

Subaltern Dialectics

For the thrill of being
almost psychotic
to you, as it were,
to shock you, otherwise,
in a nonordinariness,
you should only have
collectively trained
a deliberate disregard
for me . . . no?

Anxiety Attack

An anxiety attack:
An insensibility in a sensibility:
The world, as one knows it,
in a discrepancy
can waive itself elsewhere,
far from the self,
and not happen too often:
An anxiety attack, too,
could be said to be a challenge,
in the event
of an errant defocus--
A kind of immediate disallowance
of the right
to his own focus:
The anxiety
may yet come to be
a gratuitous abstraction
of the experience
and altogether
could be a part of
the new normality
of our times.

Solomon's Seal

A new-fangled breach
of Solomon's Seal
into that phenomenalism,
where choice could less cope,
wandering from market to market,
to founder amidst people who were far between,
or over my decisions.

My own dignity, like a black escalade, segued,
subito, I suffered a breach.
Yet by the love from whom,
I tendered the transcendental belief
of a new empathy
to make choice or flow.

Freud

Being driven,
or a stewardship of the mind,
the super-ego,
of Freud's formality--
To mean to us
in the person,
and as sleeveless in the cure,
being that necessary,
when out of nature.

Imperiling Id

Structured as a maleased feeling,
so extravagant a devilry,
a minus content surveyed
is liable unto
their own salubrious whole, which might not bear
so much fission in parts
and at risk, or rapt,
or averse, or to evert,
and sometimes excessive in whatsoever care.

Catharsis

Down with catharses!
And up with desire!:
A technical problem,
or one of
some difficulty,
can also
be met
by a *precedent doing,*
or so be in it.

Irresponsibility / Responsibility

I could desire of myself,
or even with an infirmity
and to be reprieved
by not what are overbearing responsibilities,
and can be
like a prolixity
of the words of indicia
in events
or be as lax.

Irresponsibility could also be
of what liberties
from a self's overborne duties,
yet nigh hold to conserve –
Or upend the straits of one's existence
in the self-preservation,
or the self-same fraughtness
of what events
in life.

Synchysis

A person who loves
everyone else
may have the synchysis
for his own self
and might not
incur its return in time:
The synchysis, too,
can be in your basic
interpersonal deceit.

Synchysis: confusion of words

Fantastication Hypothesis

A fantastication of the ethic
per the system of the family, a hypothesis,
to parallel Freud's seduction hypothesis,
when the noble citizens of the turn of twentieth century Vienna
would not admit of incestuous behavior,
or if Freud's patients must have had unconscious seduction
fantasies.
Some years later, Freud rescinded this hypothesis
and in our own modernity,
the civil, moneyed citizens of advanced western countries,
through their own behaviors,
may garner fantasticating behaviors,
as frequently the bevies of their own sons and daughters.

Dr. Carl Whitaker

A meaning of the logical term, ("∃"):   "There exists",
could be surmised
of psychology to mean:
'From psyche to system',
that is, from 'psyche' to the former of
'good system' and 'bad system'.
Or 'what' may infer systems,
whose sucklings remain
a phenomenal meaning of "∃".

Psychoanalysis

My psychoanalyst stilled
my Unconscious
with my consciousness.
He deliberated
his head
into my own
and bethought it
the very aid
to my so analysand's Unconscious.

The outcome of some psychoanalyses
is the unintentional
"immotion" (or the impulses)
of his patient,
the latter
to model himself
in the analyst's one-up-manship,
or if be as counter
to the society at large.

To be set unto – or after –
the so-called
age of reason of our culture,
of which in the psychoanalysis
after Freud,
being the *therapeutic*,
at large,
or say of
the fall of language.

Drive

Freud had said that the Unconscious
is fashioned like the structure
of a language.
Or, rather, it can be of sorts,
like an *unintentional modus*
of the self's motives--
Or can be found
in the portage
between the voluntary or not.

Driven

Psychoanalysis can also
be as subversive
of one's 'doing'
and phenomenologically speaking,
charging one's
psychical filigree:
My psychoanalysis
was a kind
of self's re-doing.

Do (I)

Doing can be enheartenment,
to look, then to do,
or see, then do,
in what order –
Perhaps, alike
a spiral center,
or what unconsciousness,
and that could, again, be but to do,
yet, if in the disheartenment,
perhaps, alike from what so spiral center.

Do (II)

Caring in time,
like to be the self
occupied in one's productivity,
or like a gainful bond
of instants in a clockwork.
But not agonizing
in this stance,
being if discretely,
or, that, to do.

The Analyst

My analyst "tripped" me
with his jargon
to craft
my being productive,
drawing out my intentions
to service a personation
that may have
but gone to serve only infantile ends.

My analyst apparently
could not,
more than usual,
forego a system's field
of awareness
during my psychoanalysis,
when the heteronomous theses
ought to manage the *experience*
into the capacity of the analysis.

A real consequence
of psychoanalysis
may be the analysand
becoming more
like the analyst--
that is, a model
in the former,
to be as the analyst,
or more ill-suitably interpersonal.

His semantics,
or the analyst's
own so very civil moves:
The analysand
may not see
the problem
to himself
in his own time,
or yet for himself.

A Verbal Diablerie

A long-term psychoanalysis
also can be met by a structural etiolation
in the analysand
that might saturate
onto their dialogue,
or even up to
a sort of verbal diablerie,
or being hitherto
there was an ab intra silence.

Distimed

The analyst earns his due
by his work in motley disclosures
of the analysand's "past time" Unconscious.
And should the neglect
of his 'here and now'
be avenged of his 'past time',
or which to be from his own languishing,
enough of a spiraling
in the catharsis.

Catalepsy

A human catalepsy, by degrees,
or a kind of pneumatic unreturning –
And animal motion –
should have
a kinaesthetic return.
At least, above,
requires the brink
of language,
or, respectfully, no language at all.

An unmovedness can also be inertial,
or to be captured in three-dimensions,
like the proverbial goose in a bottle –
Or through an alter want,
as the mode of escape
in the fourth dimension and fifth dimension,
can be the reversion
in the past time
and of the Unconscious.

On being as reactive
to what caveat:
"One should
have such an anxiety
to be such
a waxing slowness
of the mind,
yet for the need
of rational thought."

Anxiety (I)

Gilding in the stuff
of actuality:
The world, at times,
might seem like a hoax,
even be with a simulacral order,
as the anxiety
and the deceit
in the small,
or at large.

Anxiety (II)

Anxiety is also like
a 'clip' in time –
Or rather could
pretend to be as if
a clip in the Greenwich Observatory-
Or the latter
being to affix
a productivity
in times.

Fall Anxiety

Anxiety for some people
can be said to be
a social potentiality,
or to purport
to be a void.
Or a personal evanid-ness
may follow
the death
of so close an other.

Decompensation

Of gratuitous feelings,
or in unwitted catharses,
words, too, can be a compensation,
until the decompensation,
if that is a word,
like the minimum of a potential,
or in a system,
has converted it
unto rational actions.

Narcissism (I)

People talk to me,
or like me, here, or elsewhere,
to like myself and remain content,
that I am strictly owed in so many illimitable conversations
for the sake of my productivity
in the elongation and prolongation of myself
for a far abstraction in me,
as strung-out in the matter and in the manner
of my own personal sustenance.

Center

At the would-be center
of the mind,
or the being of
so nonexistent objects,
is to fend off
what could be a trespass,
or to avert which of
a wanton penetration,
or into another.

Words (I)

It is a challenge
to make of words,
and not be wordy,
like the heave-to
in a tug of war:
The thread of life,
the program,
and the force
of the words.

Ego

A colossus of the ego
to put down its antagonists,
or might who claims to be
larger than life,
as well, until
he holds a *monopoly*
on others' utterances,
or he ought to respond
only to himself.

Pluto

Farther on, the future appears
to be a call for
the kind of culture
of a more so-called
frigidity of sound,
or as if
this has only
which a positivity
of the future.

A Heliofugal Power

Heliofugal ways of existence
may take what one has for granted
and accept a detached existence, forever,
like machinations of power:
And you may recline,
as it runs with enough potentiality in
so plenipotentiary a system
in a matrix of whose satisfactions.

Heliofugal: tending away from the sun

Bloop

Call it a "bloop,"
on the brink of one's independence –
Devolving into dependency,
an inadvertent forgetting
of something
that has been part of
one's consciousness.
And "bloop":
Gone for the next term of time.

Warning Sounds

A freight train's horn, a distant longing,
a poignant sound,
alluding to the reflections of the human condition,
or if not so material the perception:
Yet, perhaps, something ought to be done
to this sort of "outlier"
in the capacity of a modern positivity,
when only in the stuff of afterward what ought to be heard,
but wide in its sound.

Fly by Night

The surreal depiction of myself
stopping at a railroad crossing,
wearily, in the wee hours of the morning,
when a long freight train passes,
powered by two green locomotives.
I eventually cross, arrive at home, and go to sleep.
When I wake in the morning,
that freight is transumed –
If I ponder to muse of it this way,
hundreds of miles away.

Polities

Inner Conquest of the West

Through actions of the self
and actions of another,
who suppresses the first
of a terrified ego,
adopting in that dead reckoning
a compromise
to greed, cupidity, and the transcendence,
overtopping an imperfect human social bond,
one by one,

This pattern continues,
regressing, (or in one's self, advancing)
of one's lateralness in the first place,
wishing for the conjugation
with as little of the former's
ambition on others,
or as often his selfdom.

Now collateralized with many others
through whose misease
of not getting their impending need
or recognition of the self,
within the frame of reference of the west,
is botched, the ego of the second
informed of a dead transcendence of the west,
a desecration,
like an unilateralization of influence
by the second.

This, honeycombing, again, such portions
of western culture
(started through the tradition
of Orpheus, Pythagoras, and Plato)
by ideological agents,
that second from the east
to avenge such earlier conquest
in 326 B.C.
by Alexander the Great of Macedonia
in India.

Amtrak Hotel

At Amtrak hotel
there is a little dialectic hereabouts,
a strict *constitution sans talent--*
just peace, quiet, and dignity,
and a small dialogue to note, no irony:
What are we free to do?
There is power and protection,
yet residents have little desire outward
to be sovereign.

Toward a Bauble Culture

There seems to be the coming of a bauble culture
in which doughty illusions from
internet-ordered, or popular-bought games,
provide diversions over cultural and individual worries,
replacing the real
and gaining favor
by accruing or collecting baubles
and leaching resources,
or as the tinniness of so ingenuous a population.

Affabulation

A dilemma on what is appropriate,
delineate, or a' point –
is often something too personal
for the current terminology
of modern psychology,
and yet there are half-baked fads of description
for the fantastically minded,
that can make the problem even larger,
yet not for those who live in less slaven frames of reality.

Love/Knowledge

The latter, if it be off-balance,
and the former, as freely of a situation,
then the former of the intent
and the latter, an obtainment,
of the diligence-
Yet the place
of its constancy,
or gratis,
may proffer love.

Lawrence

Lawrence differs in its progressive society
from other Kansan towns,
to be this 'do your own thing' city.
Or some people need traditional structure.
And others wish for the more unrestrictedness, or
unconstrainedness,
to find that Lawrence could be sometimes as *low*
on a stress, passion, and the possibilities of compassion,
or the levity sans gravitas.
And this northeastern Kansas city
can be as politically correct, or cliquish,
and yet free--
a bit yin,
or of the interpersonal milieu.

Some College Towns

To advance oneself socio-economically,
one seeks an informed education,
to deliberate the schools in many a college town.
Yet where there may be a partying life
among one's collegiate fellows and sisters,
there could be in contrast
a *gravitas,* or the gratuitous strain,
evidently, that seems to have
a lightness of response, sometimes, of others' likes
of uncompassionateness.

Topeka

In the legal city
of Topeka,
the state capital of Kansas,
anyone bent
on a not being egalitarian
is struck by
a lack of difference
between one's own dignity
and another's.

Here and Now

What is it
about living
in Topeka, Kansas?
Is there less
'there and then'
in my here and now?
And is my here and now
more self-evident
than not?

The Author Outside of Topeka

Dark rain clouds
to wet the soil
and the winds endured
in shuttering the windows of the big house:
The farmer's land should yield a good crop on the sunny days.
And we have no longer the need for primitive empathy for the
weather,
or for the natural way of things,
because it's all for power:
And your crop of corn should be the best this year.

The Shore of Kansas

Polluted, with debris,
and strewn awash
from an incoming ocean wave front,
or the great plains of Kansas
in the inexorable dreaming,
or perhaps in the absence
of a dream –
And the descent into what is semi-arid,
or the ebbing of a muse.

The Jerk

He who is unacceptable
and blamed
in the judgment of others
might not have others' interests--
And may be co-dependent
on the bullying of him:
They could bind him,
or be cursory about it
be as he is so low down.

Fabled

Should I, as sorrowful but noble,
exist at all?
Why don't you just fable me,
when society, at large, has the less resource for me
and about which I am not unproductive,
or the above better
than some assumption
of the former
in myself, or of others?

Early Intent

He was a sympathetic nil,
a blade of grass,
or like its shades:
And society,
being only interested
in the manner of his handicap,
and unwilling
to add that self-esteem
unto his person.

Scope

America can ignore its scopic population,
the population delegated to watch the rest,
those savvy of the state of culture,
to look down upon,
as a weakening, or an over-indulgence,
or even the acrifying of productivity.
One ought, instead,
nominally to dream, to labor,
and, resolutely, as to earn.

Hyperphasia

A reduction in living
and an attention to bodily organs:
The dependency on talking
of their life functions,
to ultimately break with life, itself,
even after the naming
for the sake of needs-
Or to gabble words of dire concern
to one another:
Yet die,
no longer to be able verbally to cavil about one's liver
to one's cronies, again,
as in the media, like on their erstwhile TV:
It is a terrible thing.

Apple

It is legitimate
for a good apple
to throw out
a bad apple
without the need for an apology.
For this is the way that uniformity
of opinion,
preceding science,
was achieved.

Sponge

Mental concavities
and a *sponge,*
or a person,
through such modern advertisements
to the many,
or from the media,
and the impinging
unto whom- and in times,
what cannot will its own movements.

Turkey

When being too talkative,
that is,
to 'gobble',
could be a program
of a turkey,
or if it should be
the animal's spirit,
or in a person.

The Origin of Rudeness

You, sir, in particular, need the very obscuring inside you,
disclosed,
for your own good.
Aren't you one of the rabble?
This, then, for your speaking with authority:
How dare you!
Your intellectual property can be vandalized at our discretion.
But how, frankly, can we live
in the more rude and crude
of a compensation for our exigent survival?

Vladimir Horowitz

Vladimir Horowitz, in a depressive phase of his life,
checks into a room of a flophouse in New York City
and after a fair night's sleep,
in the morning
opens the door to his boarding room.
Seeing a charwoman on her hands and knees
scrubbing the floor in the hallway,
he demurely asks, "Where's the piano?"
"The what?" she replies.

A Barmecidal Feast

A conspicuous rich man doesn't often give to the beggar
anything appreciable in substance,
but a possible Barmecidal feast,
a great illusion of all manner of food and drink.
This is the way of the world,
the half-way pact between the haves
and the have-nots.
Furthermore, in an envy of the contrast in culture,
a vernacular language,
together with sundry reaches and referents,
when used in excess
by the learner's tongue
becomes the biggest Barmecidal feast
of them all,
and in what circumstances
the true master should finally say, "noli me tangere",
of the crowd, in spite of themselves,
would please grant him a respectful quietus.

Barmecidal: giving only the illusion of plenty

Hearts of Ice

He, alike, vexatious
in his general infidelity,
but we are conscienables
who should feel obliged
to have him with us,
yet enough is enough,
and for the sake
of our own health and dignity,
by his company
we'll now turn him out
and seem heartless,
"when the world is like that,"
and at the very tip of a hat,
or if like the hearted paradox.

Those Remote are the Irreal

Living in the genteel North Shore of Chicago,
people believe you are what you look like, irrespective of your
history,
and they are relieved
of direct dealings with subalterns,
due to their conspicuousness,
which, elsewhere, for tax monies,
the Social Rehabilitation Services
should provide the primary contact for,
if not otherwise than:
"Sorry, we don't have an ear for losers, here.
Or I never knew you."

Provenance

I could infer from him, now in Chicago,
that I no longer
have a historical territoriality in Chicago,
for a historical claim, or the due respect:
Or, previously, I had a home, therein, for fifty years,
but now having moved:
What does that
remind you of
on the world stage, today?

Impare Uncompromising

Americans tend to dilly-dally
with each other's class
and maintain physical and emotional separability
from that poor soul,
whose needs must be met:
"I can't spend more quality time with you,
for you to act as though
you were already a shade of Hades
suspended above Lethe.
I must protect my own interests,
to live, work, and produce in lifeworld.
I am sorry that I no longer have time
to probe with you
all the stupid things
people have done to you."
(But you can't just abandon me, here, now can you?
Reply: "I sure can".)

Liberal Agenda

A liberal agenda
and a liberation from such subalternity, to boot,
in which we should prefer the veil of ignorance
between "ourselves" and "them"
for the best of all concerned:
We only want
a little exposure to them at a time
and the filter
between what they are going through and us.

A Big Catharsis for the Black Folk

Eva, a poor black housemaid in the 60's in Chicago
who cleaned our house for a nominal day's pay once a week,
took the Elevated in the morning
from her tenement building
on the south side of Chicago
to our large house in the north suburb
and left late in the afternoon
amidst the omnipresent class order,
where the white folks on the North Shore
gained their wealth,
and the blacks, when at work,
to receive their excruciations of spiritual knowledge.

Imports for the Possibility of Police Brutality

The police being drawn in to cite
what little of the law
in behaviors,
that a negative ambience
may alert the police,
in a basis for what charge
of a persistent behavioral lack,
or in the rules
of a rational civilization.

Dignity

Are dignitary rights a formalism?
Do we have the right
to be indignant, as well,
if in truth,
that does not mean
rights to a wrong-doing,
or the former
unto multiples
of meanings?

A Humiliation

A meanness in what is associated
with the over-sensitization
of a personality
is related to the denial
of a self-esteem,
or to create
the consequence
of mental, physical,
or spiritual violence.

A Civil Dread

The conceptualization of a human atrocity
can, too, be as barbaric,
when the following, if concrete, is
in common with many people,
who still believe in incivility
from a tyranny of the one self-spoken
that may begin as a little barbarity
and more afterward,
if not as *earlier-on* eschewed.

Hoax

So-called unhoaxers,
also, might tend to be as violent
toward the lying proclivities
of a world's hoax--
Or being the violent person
toward some inhabitants of the world,
who could be as "evil" hoaxers:
The former, therefore, to kill off the hoaxers,
wherever they may be.

Ignorement

The ignorement
of one, altogether:
He is the other's murderer
in the fourth degree,
or obstructed
with *alienable* rights,
or seem whose strangers,
yet be of so
inalienable rights.

Massless

Ignorement can be
the inception
of organic spirals.
"Ignorers" may be the shadows
on the wall
in the allegory of Plato's cave.
Ignorement is something
that may move,
but has not a civic momentum.

Invisibility

Of one not nominally being
in the same social frequency,
by the judgment
to leave the one,
irrelatively lost-
But if the one is saved,
or if to be near the same social frequency,
again, or when one is as unconformable,
and specifically is ignored.

Forgone Forgiveness

It is said that those who understand all, forgive all.
Yet after Modernism, there remains a mental tension
between what can be understood
and what can be gotten used to,
when of the latter, the increasing technological presence
for Post-Modern society is bound to bypass understanding,
or to suffer more angst,
and less inclined to outright forgive
than to tolerate passively.

Election

The democratic outcome
in some elections
can be the matter
of such sense of the equivalence
in each candidate's
popular or unpopular impression
unto the *demos,*
even up to
winning, or not.

In this age, when the geometry of Euclid
is not intuitive to most,
why should
the presidential bid between candidates
not tally to be near a tie?
After all, the probabilities
of the outcome of the vote
are almost like equal fashions
in the first place.

Not All Reality

For the irregarding personality
in our times,
something outside that person
could also carry
his very "inconspicuous unacknowledgment",
or when in reality,
some of those existents
and relative diminishments
may just as so disappear.

A Politic Language

In the paradigm
of social norms
a person
can communicate,
as naturally,
or as patent,
when the language
is worthy,
and in order for it to be accepted.

Yakety-Yak Fascism

His elocution
should command full attention.
Yet it has peripheral meanings,
and many have only part of an access
to the perception of years,
the chance to understand
being a punishable circumstance,
as he holds you—and you to him—for dear life
in a bombastic language
of *goofish fascism,*
to hold one to be loyal to the other
up to our ears,
and no more.

Warding the Leech

He should bait at will
to stultify others
and rid them of their desire
to work for his adversary–
or anyone's willingness to work with that one,
and to dissuade
one from the other
from any longer
putting out the effort–
The more for him
than what in preference should be only paper thin,
if, otherwise, of that let be–
You would face the anathema – or thread
to the adversary's advantage,
for here, yet boldly belied, lies a metaphysical leech!

Technocracy and a Nothingousian Influence

"Take from the nothing-ers?"

A unilaterality of positive influence,
exclusively, of the productive in society,
as the pall of unproductive influence,
its compactness, a null or negative influence,
and such chronicling no longer heard, or of interest,
like a prisoner,
regimenting the secrets
of his prison-house
and to preserve the hegemony of powers.

Negligibility

Statistical negligibles, or outliers,
are less moral
as a utilitarianism,
when not pertaining to individuals.
For when the outlier sound frequencies
of J.S. Bach Passions
are eliminated from the recordings,
they become more efficient, exact, and legitimate,
but the less radiant, or if less the human warmth.

Max

Watching a good
TV program
is a good
TV program.
And if from without,
Max can interfere
by telephoning us,
so then nigh he is a schlemiel!

"Put-up or Shut-up"

In these modern times,
when an imperative
to communicate
to others, at large,
one must
either "put up",
as adapted for TV
in likeness,
or to shut up.

Put-Down

The means
of the modus operandi,
or *to roll:*
To intend not to be
an irrational person
and the wish to be rid of,
that he, whosoever, should be
the biggest fool
of them all.

The Stinkeroos!

The very least you could do
is not to be a stinkeroo.
The stinkeroos!:
What stinkers, who can make civic life really difficult:
The tedium and levy of the day's work
and its forcible non-here-and-now',
its uncleanliness
need not be taken home,
of what nominally ought to pleasure one
in the obvious values of a deserved leisure.
For otherwise, stinkers lie and are lied to
and in an arbitrariness
without batting an eye,
not a convenient satisfaction
for the dignity
in one's own working life.

Gamesman

In the aggression
of the gamesman,
there is advised the practical conceit
of the world purported,
as too much a 'cock and bull' place
to feel overly safe or contemplative –
A discretionary reality –
So conferred on mankind
for the gamesman.

Objectification

To be cognizant of whatsoever in focus,
a gamble with life,
a tropic focus
to see a sundry variety,
then various and sundry patents,
or to imagine
a turn from an actuality, as an over-focus,
of a here and now perception,
or see not singly the one possible world.

Solitary

In the heart
of many Americans
is the desire
to be amongst those
of their own sentiments.
Or one should claim
the capacity to be alone,
or if that being
'in the dark'.

A Routine

In times of anguish,
or less the joy,
it might be best
to return,
if as craven,
otherwise, *to resume*
in the portions
of a normalcy,
or in a routine.

A Presentation's Loss

People often fail to see
the unfolding of essential values in another person,
when they themselves don't accord to the characteristics
of personal appearance and demeanor,
and neglecting other values
to face a decline of one's personal presentation.
It is possible, too, in a bias
toward one's own party
is a failure to see the presenter's own essential worth.

The Thief

A possible inference
of the thief,
who fails to have the sense of worth
in owning his own property,
for it follows
that the thief rearranges: "What is yours is yours"
and "What is mine is mine"
into the belief, "What is yours is mine",
and that appears to him true.

Straggling Ethic

A normalcy in modern America
might be the legitimation of an 'inconscient' gene,
the development of general over-focusing,
when focus and determination are thought
the innate builders of America.
But contributions of some liberal traditions
are from those who have decided to be aware,
if even ironic,
to become a straggling ethic.

Swishy Morals

As persons, often of their own behaviors,
try to keep the status quo,
they develop
an unconceptual, immoral,
ungraspable "swishiness",
or slipperiness,
in order to maintain their egotistical
configurations of societal powers
of their own social hierarchy.

Subaltern

They urge their being
instead of living it.
Their mire of ignorance
protects them in their personal space
from the lucidity
of the world, actual, or at large,
in which they present not much of a part,
as they smack only of the knowledge
relative to their own chosen cliques, and little other.

Uninsured Sympathy

In modern society,
there is not the resource of time
for everyone to be sympathetic
to everyone else
and some intended sympathy
is swallowed by the other diversions
and other patterns of events,
else eradicated
by our own cynicism.

Orwell

To make a simpleness out of complexity,
or a simple of the author:
Simple the reader.
Freedom is slavery.
Simple is complex.
It's a no-brainer!
Or one be adamant
to simple another
and bait the complex,
or the "Global Warming
is a socialist plot!"

No Exit

A diction from without
in a social protocol
arises from the media,
to act as
a 'no exit'
for so many
funky, scared,
and spelled
the populace.

Discontent

A psychical maintenance,
or threatened per a one-way
'Thanatic vampirism', that is,
what the causes of
these wide-eyed
conditions of worldly or unworldly discontent,
for otherwise, or where
there ought to be instead of
what inner peace!

Detour

In a detour,
or if liable,
can be the behavior of a
stemming out--
or is the space of a
branching out--
to save the directive's integrity,
instead of
the will's unconscienability.

Selfies

"Selfies" can also be
a "biased knowledge" of a kind,
or in the love of self.
And a pining for experience,
otherwise, could arise from a vacuity,
or the consequence
of a desire upon whosoever existence,
and being as inconscient
in their activities.

A Narcissistic Intersubjectivity

Narcissistic individuals,
with few defining concepts of others,
could leave the others intimidated.
Having no so obligatory thoughts of them–
He or she, just a formality,
and as pliable, pleased to make of them
a transcending formlessness,
like the grandeur
of self-interest,
to tower or vault above,
or invested with the very sense of himself:
Others ought to be as jealous.

Narcissism (II)

A Narcissistic person
may have the means of operation
to 'dis'(disconnect) others,
while the other
must resource himself
of himself,
or, affrontingly, has
not enough- or by a complementary demand
of the first.

To have been
Narcissistically 'disconceited'
can also be
a form of abuse:
To disconceit
the alterity
and Narcissism,
as so, could be
a heteronomy.

Logged in Cement

Stopping-up desires
by the *denominating* of that one or by *homogenizing* the other
into a social system,
if motivated to do something
from that desire,
offers a null social investment,
a bare operation:
One becomes a social protuberance
and loses his autonomy.

That Anonymous Blob over There

This man has become so nonentitled, generic, homogenized,
And as denominated,
and thus made, so specific, or anonymous, in all directions,
that we don't even want to be in the same room with him.
There needs must be space
to escape his presence,
lest we, too, become subject
to the same forces.
For, rather, we prefer the peerless authority
of our own original a promise to ourselves.

Oblivious

A lifestyle
of being oblivious,
perhaps as useful
of another's advantage
in whom lying to?
Or of the advantage, as well,
of those to the former,
as they
could lie to.

Selective Listening

In his sub-community behavior,
a person is often conditioned
to do or say
what others
have already heard
and understood of him,
dispatching him
of a little difference,
or count as nothing:
In his behavior
a person is conditioned
to do or say
only what others hear,
or understand –
To dispatch the rest,
and so risk nothing.

Unlistening

To leave the 'unfit' behind,
the emotions, et. al.
This is the essence
of a person's "transcendence",
the ideology of anything
that does not disilluminate himself
nor another like him
is acceptable
in his own illumination.
That in the passing by another,
he has an impenetrability,
an unlistening,
that obliges
his intuition instead.

Sound

"Ǝ" the aural:
In reading books,
words are also like to
the aural:
Or which,
aurally, could
motion the body –
Or, too, of the soundless,
to languish.

aural: pertaining to the ear.

Primer to a Kind of Success

The strategy in
ruthless objects of power,
less social empathy,
or less the furthering of culpability,
is like working in a successful career,
or in a corporation,
with such skills
and motivated, too, by
evitable guilt.

Conditionedness

In this Post-Modern western culture,
a conditioned reality, only, is sanctioned,
where young people are loved, simply,
because they are founts
of conditionability.
Alternately, if one lacks a conditionedness,
and is not conformably artistic,
the society believes he ought to submit
to a common treatment.

We

'The multiplication of myself'
could stymie
my individuated behavior,
yet for the exception of *society*,
or a one-dimensionality
of desire? –
With whosoever aside
to be from what objects of desire –
Or, to mark us to repel.

Automorphism

An architecture of central buildings
have their characteristics:
They have little style
to do with other buildings,
or other people,
in their surroundings, respectively,
presenting an absence of intersubjectivity,
like a godhead of difference,
or a simultaneity from within.

God's Public Relations

It ought certainly to be true
that God's diverse creatures
all have a divine dignity,
though all souls ought to be reverenced,
some have a rather
lapsarian view of things to themselves,
for which there is
a kind of management made
in God's public relations,
keeping one's private
thoughts and attitudes to oneself,
a kind of privilege,
like an authoritarian personality,
while in fact being clandestine
and keeping the invalidity of the flock
or a practical courtesy at bay by being prudent.

Non-Event

An actuality,
or an elucidation of one's sentience,
hides existentially
in the elucidation's nonresponsiveness,
to the others' unspeechfulness,
a desideratum or the want of so more facile terms from above
to what nonexpressiveness,
or altered to be like a neediness below,
and could supplant one's independence.

Barren Unsubservience

A concern of the liberating of people
is not always a pragmatic social proposition,
for not all people, by their seeming natures,
may be humanly initiated,
when some of them
have refused to improve themselves
for such and such a reason.
How can one of null subservience
be helpful to one or another at all?

Non de Profundis

Steeped as I am in these general issues,
being yet culturally relevant,
but unbeknownst to a higher society, at large,
pensive and bitter, as I may be at the present time,
what ought to still be
the issue that typically does not suffice,
nor practically pertain to currents of major concern,
or the knowledge of a higher cultural influence
in the country and in our times.

A Dismal Pattern

Some dismal patterns
of the Post-Modern era
can emerge like the allegory
of the tortoise that would ferry the scorpion across the stream
on its carapace,
only to be turned against midway across.
This already had been anticipated by the tortoise:
For if it be stung on its neck, halfway across,
both would drown.

Labels

Labeling, or the underlying of another,
to believe a practical conceit
for those to dominate,
or cast a stigma,
for which people could choose
a class of labels
over the ones to be labeled–
Or labels could be a poor excuse
for the 'knowing', or not knowing of something.

Sensibility

A verbiage "pings"
from its various media sources
and people ping
their sundry and miscellaneous
behaviors, unpredictable,
as noise to each other,
to which hoards throng to the movies,
those with guns,
and bullets ablaze.

Distraction = Experience

What is distracted from
must be real.
What is distracted by
is only sometimes real.
But what of the experience?
We need to confirm a balance
in the objectivism
and the subjectivity in such currency
of our work-a-day world.

A Neo-Barbarian Creed

To stay unto oneself
a unilateral experience,
or to keep another
a perfect stranger,
can be to speak "mentalese"--
To not have a thought, or another--
Or survive by stimulus-response
and blow out yet another candle of culture,
whenever vexed.

Connective Bonds

People of all ages
should benevolently be more connected
in the present era
to redeem the society.
But many of its present populations
have ineluctably afforded
an imminent slack,
a haphazardness,
or if it appears to be totally disconnected.

Future Shock

A management in the anticipation
of artifacts
in modern culture,
as figuratively,
of an ethereality,
or the synthetic spiral,
and be akin
to hasten
in this age of anxiety.

Offense

A valetudinarian, even though,
could be societally offensive,
or if obtains
the deeming if not societally natural,
to be relieved
of some civil duties,
as obstructive in the consequences, in degrees
of some civil disreputiveness,
or to be of what impertinence.

Valetudinarian: an ill person

A Normative Protocol

A perennial problem:
Of too many infra-dutiful persons
not tolerating
extra-dutiful people,
basing their treatment
of the latter,
as a model
in a person
with half their IQ.

Is there always
a difference
between claiming
a high IQ
and the chronicity
of having
a one-upmanship
over so very
many others?

Moonstruck, Ignore

The pursuit of happiness
in his standing belief
concerning an obliviousness of others,
their reality, or no reality:
Both can be practically
an ethical unheededness
and when being useful to him,
or solely
for his own domain.

The Scream

Less a humanity
and more a defacement
would bestill
the *scream,*
or then
by that,
a mental lag,
or that
in a stagnancy.

The Unconscious

Particularly, in America,
its Unconscious
is ill-often,
namely, a drive
of an involuntarism,
or be informed
of the derivative,
as self-clenched,
then a driving through –
Or a creative indifference
in a fantasticism,
or like the pool
of its implicit energies.

Natural Law Party (I)

Their most natural obtainment
would have the unfit bested by the fit
and the former's so-called irreversibility of floundering
should preserve the natural law
in a world of fits--
And his utmost's success,
where the fits overpeer the unfits,
yet assumably kept:
Or the unfits ought to fail the more often.

Natural Law Party (II)

To serve the so-called natural law
sees the fittest to win,
and the unfit,
yet could be
their negative due
and the way
of the fit, as well,
can end with
his own illumination of mind.

Unnatural Law

Is to behaviorally condition
an unfit person
to be even worse off,
though a kind of
'natural' in the world?
Or one to condition
the unfit person
to lose
of that an illumination?

Natural Law Party (III)

In one surmised
of being farcical,
another can infer
what is the discarding
of the first's presumption.
Or since an unfit
ought to not be an interference
of the last's illumination
and what in his doing.

Of one being surmised
not a master,
another would incur
to discard the first
of his pretense,
when the unfit would be like a lower caste,
or that there is no comparison, only a contrast
to the other's illumination,
because of his so conferred naturalness.

Planetary Black Magick

Those in whom the rationale
of otherwise warding
the ventures too near
a black hole of the ethos,
are in a jeopardy of being
socially blacked out
from an ethic 'black hole'
in perfect selfishness and deception,
he or she could become conspicuously rich
without anyone ever knowing the truth.

Ignorance and Poppies

Ignorance can stagnate the flow of the mind
or stop a discrimination of thought.
It tries to scrunch knowledge,
or darken the light of civilization,
and like the Wicked Witch of the West
espying Dorothy's exotic band
on their way to Oz:
"Poppies will stop them.
Poppies will put them to sleep."

Philosophy

Query

If man is a motive rationalization--
that is, if there are
surreptitious predications
behind everything a man does--
then of the alternative,
I am the expression,
starting from my very thoughts, my words, and on up,
beyond the itemizations of daily life,
and the doubt of a baser feeling's claim to essence.

Descartes

Descartes can have a thought
of less shadowed vortices,
inklings of analytic geometry
in the era of the modern thinker.
And not merely
his self's introspection,
in as much the abstract integrity,
not to trammel on his personal works,
but afore to exist in the *cogito*.

The Philosopher

Her argument may represent
a possible resolve
to the moral problems of the West,
that which Nietzsche sought:
Not so grossly to lose a social equality
by way of coercion,
but such knowledge
to raise a so-called nothingness
unto something.

Incomplete Enlightenment

One cannot deliberate
an enlightenment
by planned progress,
or the noble scientific method,
whose approach of intention,
or, itself, as inevitable
a *pig hanging weird piss,* *
may recur to haunt so astute a program
of its terms in the general presentation.

*A Fortean phrase coined by Dr. T. Peter Parks

Physics

Cartesian physics
is like a vortical separability
and extending
into "hard bodies",
when within
is the *cogito:*
Of the innate,
or onto
the adventitious.

If a protocol
of "what can I do?"
is the praxis
of freedom,
then a practicum
of 'spirals'
could exist
in a physical reality,
or at large.

Ether

Ether is infinity qua infinity,
a contention,
or outside of mathematics,
and so invites the quip
that physicists
can be said to be
like fish
that don't know
they are in water.

With Galileo

By Galileo,
"Nature abhors a vacuum."
And the *inexisting moving* –
Or with Zeno,
movement is
not the heartening
of paradoxes
and the immovability, again,
of a paradox.

Movement

Movement unempts the physical.

Some organic sounds,
not necessarily
of speech
and what is
of the primal difference
in states of mind
could ever be
in the precedent
to the body's movement.

What, unstylish, can be immovability.

Choice

A "soft-choice"
can also be like Freud's associationism,
and to restore the unconscious to the consciousness,
or can be an exception
to Occam's Razor.
Yet that is the more at
an "unsoft choice",
which is like to be
a mind's rational insights.

Motion

In Newton's third law of motion,
for every action
there is an equal
and opposite reaction-
Or so that
an alienate awareness,
or in a measurement of space,
can foment
a doing of sorts.

Elision

The intent
of that
which the unstopping
hypnogogia of the subconscious
or its etiolation
in an existential sink!
And be made into
a soundless immobility
of the body.

Exertion (I)

Positive exertions
can issue from them
what a distractive spiral
in their resistance,
or like a marketplace –
of besought items,
that, as the spiral, can also
be so issuant,
as if in the beginning was a spiral.

Exertion (II)

The dilemma in which
a practiced exertion
is subsequent to
a voluntary motion
of the body – or mind:
But, habitually,
a negentropic exertion
can subsequently be
in what a movement or general immovability.

Quick

An avaricious spiral is also
like its dispersion's
quick of movement
and the quick
of sound,
or yet the unquick
of movement
and the unquick be
of what sound?

"Everything is a Depiction" (?)

Reconsider psychoanalysis:
In the adjusted depiction of the psyche
to condition one
in the Unconscious mind:
Or to depict oneself,
sometimes, in the stead of acts,
if everything could be a depiction
of the Unconscious.

Or co-depictions could permit a reality
of depicters:
Or psychoanalysis should have the outcome
of an emotion of exhaustive depictions,
or partially its loss-
And, otherwise, a motion's outcome
could be in a surfeit of depictiveness.

Wittgenstein

If you had to write a letter
that you were ninety-nine percent sure the recipient would not
open,
what would you say
that could still remain sensibly unread
and yet at least not forgotten by the writer?

For isn't this the situation with a private language,
or even a semi-rational expression
of silence that Wittgenstein put
at the conclusion of his Tractatus?

Identification

An over-identification
can obtain
an inertia of the mind
of the witness:
Yet an under-identification
can foment
the mind tossing and turning,
without regard,
or an unidentifiedness could be, as so, oblivion.

In a Linguistic Communication

There are, it seems,
so inevitable the projections
in the use
of language *(langue),*
or, too, in speech *(parole):*
And we have
the choice
between what is real
and which has that transference.

The Source

The Source might draught what resources under it
to be overt to some,
yet ought <u>not</u> to be
in plain sight,
to exist
and bode the discovery
by inimical entities:
The Source
must have a pat visibility, but only to a few.

Gaia

Gaia, the deity of the earth:
Her shadow side
presents a principle
of "one-upmanship"
and to be possible
an equivalence
in order to
construe Darwin's
"survival of the fittest".

Peace

Is to provoke
any of the many
persons' nooks and crannies
of character:
Or to make them as grateful, as well?
And be as good as
to make these improvements
upon the unfavorable traits
of the world.

Awareness = Consumption

Awareness amongst animals
and people
is like consumption.
A conspicuous consumption
amongst the parvenu
means to ignore the ignored,
for, otherwise,
near a cognizance
might not be conspicuous enough.

How does Occam's Razor fare in the use of the word
'lethological'?

Occam's Razor

How does Occam's Razor
work against a person
in the field of psychology?
For in my psyche,
if I have forgotten a word or name,
I may simply account for the phenomenon
in a certainty or a simplex of my having forgotten.
Or if I do forget,
I might tackle my memory
by taking it to be, at least associative
of the blank,
when it might be, of what image,
but from a 'razor of time' out of a variety
of the mind's processes
and to select or locate the missing word or the name for me.

Memory

When can a clinical assessment
of someone
be a sort of amnesia
of his own reminiscent accounts,
at large,
or the opposite
of the clinical,
when a tale or story
is history?

Spiral

A spiral can be an 'invariant intercalation'.

Are spirals like a demand of nothing?
And could in some hearts,
also, be like
an intentive spiral
of which
"$\rho = a*\theta$".
And as an
inorganic spiral
can be the locus
of such cleft movements.

Unminded

When not given an identity of sorts,
with less of the gestalts,
of a mental lag,
and the mind without motion,
like a specific void,
or to consider
the mental obtainment
of its
spiral center.

The Known

To follow only in the Gnosis
Of one's self-interest,
or to believe everything is behaviors,
to be practical in the world,
in life's duties,
over the ignoramuses in the world
and in what one may prefer to do,
like faring subsequent
of the knowing.

Vortex

To 'do' in practice
can precede looking.
And a vortex can be
a seeing
on the other side of doing,
or when the doing
can also be
to have as impulsive as in
what alienate's drive.

Mind's Tricks

When the mind malingers,
it resists,
or as the mind's
summary of reaching
in a notoriety of language,
a nuanced liberty of the mind,
or that it may fashion,
but not fit
of one's faculties.

Words' Tricks

Words might trick us,
or to subvert us,
when they are of bonds to us,
but not to ebb as fast
to the world:
The words
in their inveterate tracks,
and of circumstances
can harden the heart.

Words can trick us
into believing they can have
a 'one-up' of one's attitudes,
and if our empathy does not
out-event the words?
Or then the trauma of having been "de-railed"
is not, as well, always re-railed by the words,
or to come out short
in a verbal defixing.

A Beginner in Mathematics

For a beginner in mathematics,
to contemplate mathematics
without its practice
is like a diverting
in its nuances—
Or befitting the therapist,
who analyzes the bumbledom
on the spurious spooling of the mind,
but to mathematics—is unnecessary.

Nongarrulous Mathematics (I)

The garrulity of many psychologies
could also oppose a mathesis (mathematics).
And mathematics
can be a nongarrulity
of which there are links
to a span of concentration,
and a belief
in a being
of one's decisions.

Nongarrulous Mathematics (II)

If mathematics is like to
a manifold in silence,
or a symbolic language,
the words
of a garrulity
could hold the possibility of trampling
over the mathematic's inventions,
or in an ambiguating of intuition
and the seduction of language.

Either Mathematics or No

Psychoanalysis- or a dysnomy in mathematics:
These respective viewpoints
could agonize in divers practices-
On a subconscious level
of blanched contrast
to mathematics–
Or of poetry could be said
to be the very least,
of what is axiomatically composed.

A Psychoanalyst's Mantra

Consider how much
of a possible mathematizing
is being human,
or in humanism.
And mathematics is a perspicience.
Or mathematizing is a prospicience.
And the psychoanalyst's mantra
for himself—or of the mathematics
is 'conspicience'.

Posology

Mathematics could be an infinite 'pose'.
Or a symbolic synchronization
with the above
to the mathematics:
Herewith, words could also "clamour"
to a symbolism.
Or countering the repose
of heterologies,
and be as intent, throughout.

A Difficulty

A patience for the essence
may be prior to science.
And the difficulty establishing
one's own
frame of reference
bespeaks the wrangling,
as an art,
with words, brush, or tone,
not science.

In such stumbling
to try to resolve
an abstract problem,
as varied the difficulty,
he, too, must have a precursor
of an existence in an impersonal being,
with its own conventions,
or that can accrue,
still to be himself after infancy.

Symbol

Symbols press in everywhere,
like an actor
on parole.
In particular,
mathematics is like
a symbological concision
with a symbol's informing-
Or, say, informing
in a spiral's center.

Zeno

Of antiquity,
in the race
between the tortoise
and the hare,
both are individuals.
And implicitly possible
is an individuation
in the former
that passes the latter?

A coincidence of clipped events:
Or with Zeno
is the 'clipping' of distances
in that race
But de facto in physical laws
and of the continuum,
such laws of the finish
must coincide
with said laws of the start.

In the paradox of Zeno,
if not to pass
between the tortoise
and the hare, where of this
would-be event,
can engender
a logical fantasticism-
Or as consequent,
of such an astringent simultaneity.

The Dialectic

Thesis, antithesis,
and synthesis:
This, too,
can be
an obtension
of the dyad
unto the triad,
and if not
to be a category mistake?

Words or Symbols

Strictly speaking, to be words
over symbols,
could sometimes
be as lethal.
Or in the far future,
the words
in languages
of nations, as well,
may become implodents.

Is

The copula, "is",
or also
your basic
synaesthetic (?) relationship.
Or when,
throughout, therefore,
at large,
in a kathenotheism
to the One.

Words (II)

Words in embryo
or in evolving,
and words' invention
per the tribes of mankind
to mark their differences,
so we can distinguish
one word from another:
That is, in another way,
or like a *henipoeia.*

henipoeia: a number of things considered as one

Words (III)

'Words do not':
Or to condition the
generality of
a not-doing,
or the words,
after being a protology, at times,
can be as distracting, or not,
and from one's voluntariness,
or be so basic of the motivation.

Words (IV)

To solely be confined
to the words
sans their numbers-
Or like the proverbial
"bridge over water",
Or when a scientist
may find himself
in the height
of irony.

Dictionary

An 'over-tendered' dictionary of words
can also intend
the sorts of
concavities of
the space
it occupies.
So, a dictionary is like
a sort of convexity
of concavities.

Dictionariform

Or so, a dictionary of languages
is like
in its content, or its terms,
a tome
of "acataleptic impressions",
or "rational strings",
while its references, too,
could constitute
in an extrusive science of life.

Other

To hold sway
over the other,
or to try to convert
him (or her), if onto
words in a dictionary,
and to 'read',
or to put
the one
you have, aside.

"Ǝ" (There Exists)

To Karl Menger

Ǝ, or which
a thing,
or its referer,
are not necessarily decidable-
between the two-
And in the mind,
in what decisions,
to bear the thought
of a mind or the body.

Relativism

First, a relativism
in the mother's womb
of a loving psi:
Afterwards is the mother's tongue
in speech:
A sumptuary nominalism
(and its logic),
is not
all that bad.

Music

Amongst so many
other arts,
music could be
a series of such
replete of individuals of talent:
And Mozart is the best
of the earthy
and Bach,
the best of spirit.

Of Some Ego

One cannot get from 'A' to 'B'
without any mediate bias.
Non-Eucldean geometry can claim
the uniform abstraction of this 'bias',
or when the freedom from any ego
could result in a conversion,
that, for instance, Van Gogh's unbiasedness
of his art's subjects
to be a last of his ego.

Clockwork

A clockwork brain
in a time less a biological process
than the objectivizing of the mind
may result in a bit of crankiness,
that might better be tempered
by making more time,
rather than a madness
of one no longer wishing to live,
because of the banausic determinism of the machines.

Forgettery

Some machinery with quasi-human extensions to use
of their functions
can also be of our forgetfulness,
and today's current cultural progress,
or in missing time
is like a 'glass forgettery':
What machines are not lenient.
And computers
still are stuff.

Time (I)

Of one's rational sense of a time passed,
or time-consciousness
per one's own –
Like a being
in his *production*,
the *breathing*--
if to be the breath
in one producing,
or that it be of one's awareness?

Time (II)

The upside of living by the clock,
in addition to be
as gainful of linearizations
in time's increments,
or, too, could be
a behavioral constriction
in they, who again must
be like to a clockwork
in what matter's productivity.

Time (III)

The presumption
of absolute time
and an absolute history
of the world:
Such processes
would be obstructive –
Or to the precedents –
And so there being
the causes?

Kinds of Freedom

Positive freedom
is also an illimitability
in infinity,
or, perhaps,
as random a variety-
And negative freedom
is an illimitability
in the infinitesimal,
or like to be a singleness.

Hacked Language

A language, to further the syntax
of agreement in the realities of society and place,
might now advance in abstractions,
yet the illusions of non-words,
or that to obfuscate, reify, or fashion,
and the over-use of these words,
like a faddish over-reach
for the sake of a putative advance
of this era of communications,
is often bypassed
by the new-fangled language,
that can stop progress from realizing itself
in abstractions
or through the hindering of its symbols.

Dosage

Mathematics and the dosology of verbiage
are opposites in the intellect,
with the second elusive of an abstract core,
like the nonabstract dosology often found
in psychological subjects.
Jeremy Bentham called mathematics a posology,
a determination of dosage or quantity.
And mathematics more
a practical aporia.

An Uncontemplative Modernity

An adjustment,
the tendency to alleviate reality
by adjusting the vicariousness of it,
instead of extending or intending oneself
to the nature of things, as they are,
at some point of mind and soul
with a nominal judgment
that provides a convenience to many people,
who should prefer to hunker down
with a fuzzy assessment of things,
apparently yielding a concept of reality,
yet of half-dreamed up situations
and the various and sundry
of so fabulous resolutions.

Want

To live in want
can also be
a gerontological concern,
or be like
'The *center* of the spiral',
that cannot be seen(!)
But of the 'wanted',
and the 'wantedness',
may, too, be related to a voluntariness.

Sometimes, "A word is a want",
or in that linguistic,
a bid for contentment
of one's wants-
The less to suggest
a superfluity of words,
that, sometimes,
in "A want is a word",
to be the less savvy.

Mantra

Not a sort of Cartesian meditation
to think, per se,
that when practiced twice daily,
and together with
its demi-god mantra,
like in
the cosmos—
and the ego
that should be to section it.

Behaviorism

A stimulus-response
behavior that is normed in its station
and blanched of its transcendence-
In every process in time,
if to pretend in its behaviors
to be a vector in uses of language,
or there may be
the language usage's mendacity.

Behaviorism, as a most general theory,
was disproved by Noam Chomsky
by showing that it could not account
for all of our language usages,
but for the true believer,
a behavior can assert itself, again,
to instill language with such lies,
or to keep track
of them.

Such a behavior,
can also agonize zero,
or to infer zero
from the nothing–
A logical error:
And 'nothing' could, too, be
a behavior,
yet zero is not.

Socio-Physics

You do your thing
and I do my thing,
whether be simultaneous,
or not.
And if we meet,
it is an event.
And if not,
the reality of that contingency
is almost negligible.

Simplex Contact

Say, a man perceives his environment
mainly through his eyes.
Or, as he has a simplex contact,
that, a latent synergy from the five senses:
Can he be assumed as limited,
or protected in the perception
of his being enclosed in four walls?
Rather, his simplex contact suggests that
he may be sub rosa in the possession of an otherness
by a perceptive actuality.

Intuition

The author may wish
to exercise
the possibilities
of his intuition-
A sort of
tapping in an instantaneity,
or for, otherwise,
his works
can be as impenetrable.

An idea

While it is raining outside,
that in a room within a large house, but without windows,
a person can believe that it is not raining.
However, if he has an intimate intuition
without a factual evidence of rain outside,
this could also be called
"channeling", for as clearly exhorting and not with the immediate
empirical evidence,
to suggest that the ideas (or Plato's forms)
are instantaneous,
or through the medium of a possible ideal of an ether.

Group System

When outside of Rome,
do what the Romans do, anyway,
and in the translation,
of which
to others
is **not** being,
at large,
the straightness of an individual –
And there be an order to do just that.

L'arrivée

"Reaching out", as the verbal phrases,
or the declining of its present usages
in American English,
is an example of a social construction –
Or like an "unawares" way to be
of responsible behavior,
perhaps, a positivism,
and, again, a rapprochement,
To yet not be all there is.

Wooziness

A time-consciousness or time-piece,
can subduce
in the very 'saturnine wooziness",
while even
that wooziness
is a matter,
and yet
is but in
a steeled surround.

Consciousness Enigma

You've the freedom of expression, or not,
to express anything at all-
And is your choice.
But your silence
may be an enigma
to others:
A consciousness in the unspoken-
Or if the sort of noncommunication
to be of one unto another.

Contemporaries

To some contemporary milieu,
philosophy has
come to seem
as appalling to
our more
a commercial
currency - of
our own presence of
thought and behavior.

Animus

Rags of a mooning helix,
encapsulating the self:
Mercurius animatus
is often presumed
of utterances
in the offing,
or bypass whither purpose,
profit breath,
rather, aye, to *weird* the dutiful center.

Post-Modernism (I)

Post-Modernism may be so,
because determinism up to modernity
has run interference of a culture's progress.
Ethos, therefore, goads the flow
that is anti-pole to a linear ideology.
And what is ideated could cower
before the immanence
of the mind's *neural* reality,
and sap it.

The Cave

Some so-called
'pedagogies of words'
are like realities,
being projected
on the wall
of Plato's cave:
But those shadows
are not interpersonal.

A world onto the wall
of Plato's cave
and its shadows
of juxtaposed objects,
at large,
but the latter
do not "see" each other,
or less the sensibilities
of a one, specifically, to the other.

The Painted Bird

The book "The Painted Bird", by Jerzy Kosinski (1965),
was a best seller in its time,
though not a factual account, or all autobiographical,
but like a picaresque myth, sometimes true, of the bold,
wandering, sympathy-less drama,
or in the literature of a generation following Hitler,
of a person, a survivor, who must provide
for himself, by himself,
or by his own human potential,
and of his own self-responsibility.

Non-Centrifugal Mathematics

"Let None But Geometers Enter Here"
(on the entrance to Plato's academy of Athens)

When not in the midst of discovering anything,
this mathematician may humble himself
of a compass of himself not pertinent to society.
And when he does have a cogency to a result discovered,
he may find himself, indeed,
important to society
for his own relation to mathematics,
and it seems he could make himself by his task
relevant to the world.

Mathematicians are not,
generally,
a people's people.
Similarly, poets
are not usually
mathematicians'mathematics.

Fates

Clotho could be said
to be the Fate,
(from Greek mythology),
which could forward a mathematics –
Or the look of a 'clip' of Lachesis:
In Lachesis, that is,
in what *analyses* –
Or of Atropos,
when to leave the mathematics.

The Fisher King

The Fisher King of the Parzifal legend
would fish in his days in a lake nigh the Grail Castle,
or his Unconscious- in his healing
of what could neither kill nor heal,
is fit of the unconscious of the castle:
His kingly tasks could be restrained
in what consequences
of his Onanism,
and in spite of his unmarrying bond.

Swift

In 'A Modest Proposal',
the English satirist
Jonathan Swift suggests
to the superfluous Irish children
being sacrifices.
And the irony is
the people who could prosper
from Swift's proposal
are the social ends of a ruling class.

Ayn Rand

Cf 'Atlas Shrugged':
On my expectation
of Atlas
holding me up,
re: as the figure of the father.
Or, instead, a jealous brother
might provoke me,
or put me down, as meanly,
or almost every time.

Cynicism

A possible remedy
for an anxiety
is a distracting cynicism,
or in the way of two fellows in a boat,
and as imminently,
the pounding of waterfalls, ahead,
with their boat in what time left,
to take to themselves,
and be involved in a game of chess.

Whisk

Such an acceptable poem
in these pages of mine
could be likened to the repose of
cronies' hands at cards
in the game of *Whisk*,
that was oft played,
(cf Gauss in the 19th century),
after a strenuous day, (or night),
of the mathematics,
or at the observatory.

The Author: A Nuance

A true passion
has been in the trying
of words, as expressed
in figures and the sound,
which precedes it,
or the poetry,
in the communally begotten words, if discrete-
nearly of indefinite misbegotten words in the poetics,
or in those nigh the dictionary, as well.

Poetic Techne (I)

There are people,
who, leaning on culture,
yet to view poetry
as a reprieve
from a nothing-ing,
or in our everyday lives
and in our feelings,
poetry can be like a guide
amid the wondrous.

Poetic Techne (II)

A poetry could also be
like a sort of
"specious mathematizing",
and the would-be art,
as a compensation,
or if so,
our being more
so hearty
in that creation.

Less of Subjectivity

Poetry, also, can be like to lean toward
a pure subjectivity,
or if the mathematics,
being metered, or implicit,
a time-piece-
Or the latter
can also be sublimated in mathematics,
and even as
the Greenwich Observatory.

Geographic Poetry

Poems can be composed
of a deva's wonderment–
Or even in an ignorance
to be considered a place,
where people have a sufficient sight
in their compositions
to be of places
in the extensions and intensities
of the world.

A Poetic Patent

A caveat, a corroborative poetry,
as a fashion of
another's style,
or have been so held in
one's elementary school-
A *patent,*
like a self-improvement,
or, at large,
and in the symbols' realization.

And a caveat, a corroborative language
mastered in
elementary school,
still does not
perform, but later,
or as in college courses,
say, the *calculus,*
so have from
what an aforesaid convention.

A Muse or Not

Can poetry coincide
with the subconscious
of the mathematician,
or both of which,
being an expression
in their own right?
Or should poetics 'usurp' the mathematics,
and so often when mathematics, too,
may ban the poetic muse?

Strophe

Spoken, hitherto,
the words
in the dictionary
may be a go-between
of their words'
implicit dialogues,
or in
such stanzas
of poetry.

Technocracy

Would the computer contend only in a facticity?
Yet if a computer
is numerically accurate
up to 'p decimal places',
it follows that
a set of numbers, as say, above,
compares to a set of sets of numbers –
That the factitiousness
can be a sort of mal-vibration.

Prelation

The difference between a person
and a computer
is the latter's sometime
inorganic indifference to the former's
difference of the words.
Or of the computer,
the word 'prelacy'
has only the conceptual
meaning of 'prelation'.

prelation: the setting of one above another.

pc

Personal computers
can also be
the flim flam
of interpersonality –
or be
the subrogating
of human empathy –
Yet, can pc's have
an intrinsic
"be here and now"?

The labor of a straited thought,
or the leaning and usage
of a (logical) coding in pc's
could also be
an interference,
or a sacrifice
in the development
of human empathy,
or the disallowance of spirit.

A Modern Normality

A modern mankind
can create a "new normal",
a cross-hatching
of its reality onto nature-
Or a 'new normal',
which may sometimes
be said onto us
of whose **limitations-**
Or also in the work of the latter electronics.

Post-Modernism (II)

The affect
of *irritation*
could be
an indication
of lost time,
or, sometimes,
be a lagging in a relation
between man and woman
and technology.

Cardinal Time

Greenwich Observatory in England
proffers the equitable distribution over times
for production and reference:
But what of time's anticipation,
even of a possible unease, when time is not the inlook,
or is the singular time,
and its outcome,
being an allocative world,
or in physical life's very expectations.

Pygmalion

Where is the Pygmalion image's own art?

A computer may also be
as juxtapositive,
or to be set.
And as nonjuxtapositive
could be an art,
or be inventive:
And in the former
used as a model,
that the one may mimic himself.

juxtapositive: an aside of
nonjuxtapositive: not an aside of

Solvent

Money and Freedom

Positive freedom becomes, when asked,
"What stops me?"
It is motivation toward, or better production–
And money is 'stored labor', according to Marx.
The negative freedom, asks,
"What am I free to do?",
or less the motivation, less the money,
to indicate less a freedom,
or less production.

Argentocracy is rule by money
and freedom in developed countries requires money,
which affords one the exposure
to things of value.
Money in late capitalism
is no longer merely stored labor,
but amended to
that, e*n block*,
a reality, (or irreality).

Time and Money

Binding to times
to give to
our children,
or from their
parent's money:
And our adulthood
should charge us our time
and our own money
in turn.

Massman

A relinquishment of individuality,
also, is the capital
for sometimes, as stupid, the massman,
or that of a herd,
yet which of
a first motive,
therein, and one of many,
as appealed to,
or who has an unreal character.

Some consumption
in western nations
is often
by a capital
for the massman,
as those who are implicitly bound
to capitalism,
but for a sequence
of what is economically real.

Waged Existence

Of one's very capacity
to earn money
and sometimes
more often
than not,
is through
the times
of so alienative
a drive.

To have done, or should be,
in what having
an impulsive
alienation of drive:
To earn wages,
yet even
amidst anxiety,
again, may be as
solely alienate of this drive.

For one's power,
in spite of such a potential malaise,
or if to draw off another's sentience,
while he would not have –
as otherwise,
so waged an existence –
or in a late capitalism,
of one's wages,
or as often be.

Existenz

Women respect
a waged existence
in men,
or that in America,
when, at large,
there tends
to be more,
as much
so unwaged existenz.

Women

Jess

Fantasy, instead of place, is resistance,
for when I am on the other end of a phone line of late,
there seems to be some irritation on your side.
For I have called
just as you are about to repast, or when you are expecting
another phone call,
or you needs must to go to the washroom.
From illness has come the notion that I am as blanched to
insubstantiality,
instead of the person, the friend you've known for years,
and who has loved you, who loves you now, and
who still wishes you space, despite your jeopardy, to grow.

Jane

Of some people, and in my personality,
is perceived in the span of my personhood:
To some it is officious,
or if even offensive, or superfluous –
As others, mean or jealous of my intellect:
But to Jane, indeed, Jane,
I am doting
on her lovely parity with me,
or to become our commonality of likes' invisibility.

Jan

An over-sensitized personality,
veiled in ignorance from the self,
has the *aura* of a refrigerator,
irrespective and dissociated of the object.
As a person,
from the *muscles* of your logic,
you needs must have a new refrigerator,
the old one disposed, yet through a faulty logic
of the refrigerator-like, or in transference:
Had I not become warm to you
in the way you had want of me?
Or had I become as habitual
for the same reasons,
and you to maintain the apparent wish in my disposal?

Moon War

Was I on the earth's side
of Joan's singing audition?
What kind of risk
can't she reckon I took to telephone her?
Dianic? Yes.
Nary the sun.
For you would have it reversed,
or I, eclipsed by the moon,
in the umbra of your afterlife.

Ann's Offertory

On this summer afternoon in Berkeley in 1987,
Ann, being as votive,
clasps in her hands the $15
her brothers had just given her.
The occasion is
a reprieve,
however brief,
from her now so often slavish life,
or what persists in her sparing needs.

For Carole

In a congeries of her muses
of her goodness –
She is challenged, too,
by the repugning,
or oft a rejecting of the *uncaring*
for the sake,
to be as humane a dutifulness
and her upholding
of being as ethical a personhood.

Zombology

In whosoever lame use
of his personal qualities,
a nuisance to her,
or from the past-
Now I am a bug-bear,
as stupid a man,
even as perdu, lost
in the bottomless pit:
Yet I still have my anodyne.

Men!

It is the observation
of the writer
that some American women
like to 'cook' their men
in their tentative maleness,
or, that is,
by their own
women's libidinal sadism.

Let a man cook in his own despicability for a period of time
and not give him so much heed to rehabilitate himself,
until it is all a *fait accompli.*
And it is a favorite women' s gambit,
to be rid of such men, of unwanted suitors, and their ennui,
or a stillness of mind games between them,
for one of the few games
an average American woman can win at
and become free.

The Unfabled Woman

I have such mixed feelings,
when I am around her,
that she seems fantastic.
I always approach her
with a neutrality,
for if she, being as obese, or spontaneously were to explode
into a thousand pieces of jello,
it probably wouldn't
make any difference to me.

A Consequent Consumerism

In the later consumerism
of a western capitalism
a woman can learn
to answer as well the man,
though she had been secondary to men,
now in the modern protocol,
she must proffer herself,
sometimes in a duplicity,
as an ongoing temptation,
a tease per the consumerism of men,
or her message of elusion.

Women (I)

Women can over-care
about their infants,
yet wary
in the idea
of an over-caring for their infant
by a complete stranger.
For it is a vast vulnerability,
or in a jeopardy,
she could be receptive of.

Marie

To abide in a forested
far northern woodlands,
no longer
of the polity's rabble
from the south:
She is protected
and free
by the peacefulness
of the north.

Women (II)

Women of society
are such stewards
who could effectually regiment a proper
sense of reality.
It is suggested,
after all, in the manifestation of social bonds
that the character of relational bands
of people in society
become akin to our sense of reality,
for not necessarily is the reality
generated only by the facts of the earth,
or given to us from the beginning of time,
but it also has evolved through social and historical constructs of
culture,
and those systematic deterrings of "unexquisite" social bonds.